SCIENCE WORLD

ENERGY
AND HEAT

KATHRYN WHYMAN

Franklin Watts
London • Sydney

© Archon Press 2003

Produced by
Archon Press Ltd
28 Percy Street
London W1T 2BZ

New edition first published in
Great Britain in 2003 by
Franklin Watts
96 Leonard Street
London EC2A 4XD

Original edition published as
Simply Science – Heat and Energy

ISBN 0–7496–4965–8

Design: Phil Kay

Editor: Harriet Brown

Picture Researcher: Brian Hunter Smart

Illustrator: Louise Nevett

Printed in UAE

A CIP record for this book is
available from the British Library.

CONTENTS

INTRODUCTION

Everything we do needs energy. Running, cycling, eating, walking, singing, reading a book, or even sleeping – all these actions use energy. We need energy to heat our homes; a jet plane needs energy to push it through the air; a train needs energy to pull its carriages along the tracks; a bird needs energy to flap its wings. Energy is constantly changing from one form to another.

Heat is a way of moving energy from place to place. Heat always moves energy from a warm place to a colder place. A hot substance has more energy than a cold substance. A hot substance can give out heat energy to warm its surroundings.

In this book you will find out what heat and energy are and where the energy on our Earth comes from. You will learn that energy can never be made or destroyed.

WHAT IS ENERGY?

People use the word 'energy' to describe how they feel. Someone who feels tired may say, "I have no energy today". But in science 'energy' has a special meaning. It is a measure of how much 'work' can be done.

Whenever we push or pull something that moves, we are doing work. And when we do work we use energy. You use energy when you push open a door. Some activities, such as running, use a great deal of energy.

Machines also do work. A mechanical digger can move big piles of earth and rubble. It gets its energy from the oil and oxygen burned in its engine.

Whenever your body moves you use energy.

A mechanical digger at work

THE ENERGY CYCLE

All the energy on our Earth comes from the Sun! Before we use the energy from the Sun, it goes through many changes. Often when energy changes it is 'transferred', from place to place. How does the energy we need reach our bodies from the Sun?

Every time we eat food, energy is made available to our bodies. The energy comes from the chemicals that make up the food. Bread is made from a plant – wheat. Energy from the Sun makes wheat grow. With sunlight, the wheat can combine water and carbon dioxide to make chemicals which eventually end up in our bread. Energy we get from meat originally came from the Sun as the animals from which we get meat ate plants. This transfer of energy is all part of the energy cycle.

The food chain

Wheat takes up water through its roots. Its leaves absorb carbon dioxide. In sunlight, the wheat can turn these simple ingredients into sugar, starch and oxygen (a process called photosynthesis). Sugar and starch may either be stored in the grain or used to make the plant grow. The food in the plant is passed on when an animal eats it. This transfer of energy from the Sun to animals, via plants and oxygen, is called a 'food chain'.

Harvesting a crop ripened by the Sun

ENERGY CHANGES

Sometimes it may seem as if energy is 'lost' or 'used up'. But in fact energy is never made or destroyed – it just changes from one form to another, or is moved from one place to another.

Energy from the Sun can be transferred to our food. But the Sun's energy may change in other ways too. When the Sun shines, some parts of the air get warmer than others. The warmer air rises and the cooler air rushes in to take its place. This moving air current is called wind. Wind is a source of energy and can be made to do useful work. For example, it can be used to move the sails of a windmill. The moving sails can also do work. They can turn parts of a machine, for example, to pump water to irrigate the land.

Sound

When you hit a drum, the energy of the falling drumstick is transferred to the drum skin. The skin moves up and down (or vibrates). Peas placed on the surface of the drum show this clearly. The energy of the drum skin is, in turn, transferred to the air to make sound.

Energy from the wind drives the sails of a windmill.

POTENTIAL AND KINETIC ENERGY

Imagine you are holding a weight. If you drop the weight, it can do work. It might dent the floor. If the weight does work, it must have energy.

Before it falls, the weight has 'potential energy'. As it falls, it gets closer to the ground and has less potential energy. But energy is never lost – the potential energy has changed into the movement, or 'kinetic energy', of the falling weight.

An archer shooting an arrow does work on the bow to make it bend. The bow then has potential energy. As soon as the archer lets go of the bowstring, this potential energy is transferred to the arrow, giving it kinetic energy.

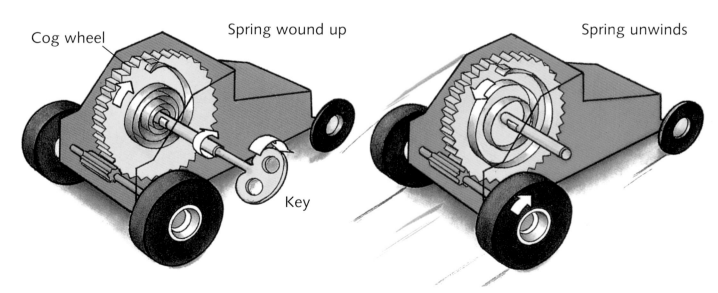

Cog wheel   Spring wound up   Spring unwinds

Key

Springs

Springs can be made to do work. The diagram shows how a spring in a clockwork car is wound up when the key is turned. Once the spring has been wound up, it has been given potential energy. As the spring unwinds, its potential energy is released and it provides kinetic energy for the turning wheels. The clockwork car then moves off.

The archer creates potential energy by pulling the bowstring.

BURNING

Another example of an energy change occurs when a substance catches fire and burns. You can make a fire by rubbing two dry sticks together. The work you do on the sticks provides them with energy and makes them hotter. Eventually, they will catch fire, or ignite. As it is very awkward to start a fire in this way, we usually use chemicals. When the match is 'struck' against sandpaper, the chemicals get hot and ignite.

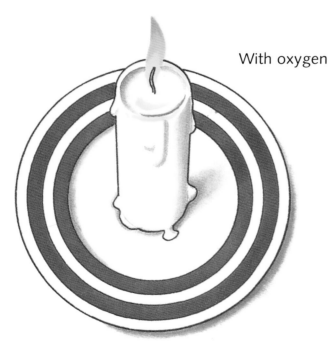

With oxygen

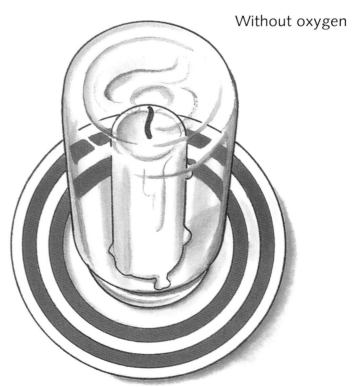

Without oxygen

Things cannot burn without oxygen. Air contains oxygen and the wax of a candle uses some of this oxygen as it burns. If a jam jar is placed over the burning candle, the flame soon flickers and goes out. Once most of the oxygen in the jar has been used the candle can no longer keep alight.

When a substance burns, energy changes and is transferred as heat. The substance itself also changes and cannot be changed back again. This type of change is said to be 'irreversible'. Fire, therefore, as well as being useful can be destructive; it can destroy buildings, damage forests and kill living things. Reducing the temperature of a fire, or depriving a fire of oxygen, can put out the flames. Other materials, such as sand can also be used to smother fire and dampen the flames.

Water and foam are used to put out a fire by depriving it of oxygen.

FUELS

A fuel is something that releases energy as it burns with oxygen. Coal, oil and gas are fuels which come from the remains of dead plants and animals and are called 'fossil fuels'. Fossil fuels took millions of years to form and can't be replaced once they've been used up. Energy from the Sun is transferred to plants as they grow. Coal is formed from dead plants. When it's burned some of the Sun's energy is released again as heat.

Crude oil is found deep below the Earth's surface and is refined before it is used. Many fuels, such as petrol, can be produced from crude oil. Substances that can provide nuclear energy, such as uranium, are also used as fuels.

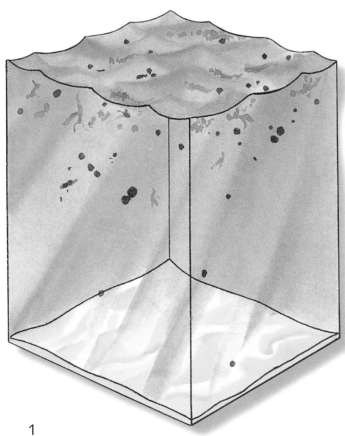

1
Silt and sand

A short history of oil

1. Millions of years ago, tiny plants and animals, different from those that exist today, lived in the sea. Sunlight, water and minerals allowed the plants to make chemicals. The animals fed on these plants.

2. When they died, the plants and animals sank to the sea bed. There they became trapped by layers of silt and sand.

3. The silt and sand slowly changed into rocks which pushed hard on the remains of the animals and plants. Buried deep underground, these remains became very hot and eventually turned into oil or gas.

Oil rigs drill deep underground.

2
Remains of plants and animals

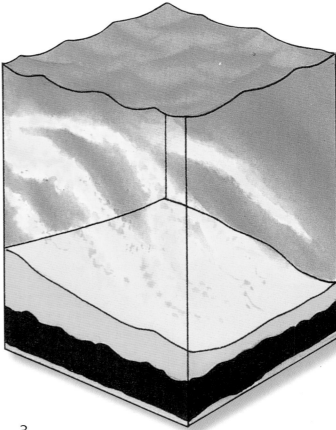

3
Silt and sand changes to rock

HEAT

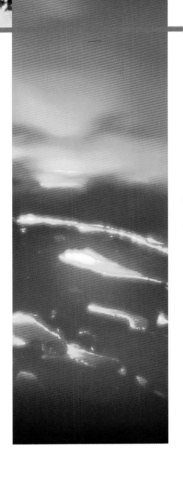

Heat is a way of moving or transferring energy from place to place. Heat always transfers energy from a warmer place to somewhere cooler. For example, the energy in a hot drink moves from the drink to the cooler air surrounding it.

Heat can travel in three different ways. When land warms the air above it, the air rises and this upward movement forces cooler air to take its place. Heat is being transferred from one place to another by moving air. This type of heat transfer, which takes place in both gases and liquids, is called 'convection'. In a solid, heat is transferred from the hottest point, along the solid, to the coolest point. This is called 'conduction'. Heat from the Sun reaches us by travelling across space by 'radiation'. Radiation is the only form of heat transfer that can occur across a vacuum.

Convection
Water at the bottom of the pan gets hot first and rises. The arrows show how the water forms a 'convection current'.

Conduction
If heat is transferred to one part of a knife from a source, it will spread out along the metal blade in both directions.

Radiation
Heat travels from a bar fire mostly by radiation. Energy is transferred as a 'ray' which spreads out in all directions.

Convection currents help parachutes to stay in the air; heat transferred by conduction melts metal.

The Sun's rays warm us by radiation.

TEMPERATURE

We often want to know exactly how hot or cold something is. We call this its 'temperature'. The temperature of our bodies is 37°C (98.6°F), except when we are ill. Even though the air around us is often cooler or warmer than 37°C (98.6°F), our bodies stay at the same temperature. This is not true of some animals, such as reptiles and fish. A lizard's body temperature may vary depending on its surroundings.

Materials are affected by temperature. Many substances can exist in three different forms; as a solid, liquid or gas. When water freezes at 0°C (-32°F) it forms ice, a solid. If water is heated to 100°C (212°F), at sea level, it will boil and quickly form water vapour, a gas.

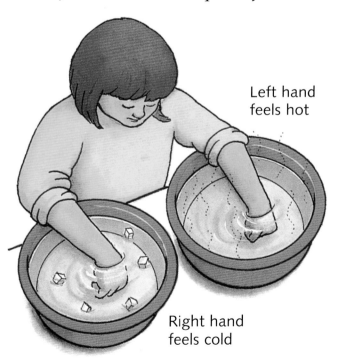

Left hand
feels hot

Right hand
feels cold

Left hand
feels cold

Right hand
feels warm

Water at room temperature

Our skin can feel whether something is hot or cold but it cannot take accurate temperatures.

Different parts of your skin may even give you different information about the same bowl of water as in the example above.

MEASURING TEMPERATURE

Temperature can be measured using a thermometer. Digital thermometers are widely used today. They give a digital reading of temperature in either degrees Centigrade (C) or Fahrenheit (F). The temperature reading it gives in melting ice is 0 degrees Centigrade (C) (-32 degrees Fahrenheit (F)) and the reading it gives in boiling water is called 100°C (212°F).

Strip thermometers can be also be used to measure temperature. They are held across the forehead. Chemicals inside the strip change colour to indicate the temperature.

The 'geyser' (above right) occurs because water running deep in the Earth boils. As water boils it expands. The water is then forced to the surface where it can shoot up many metres into the air.

Icebergs (below right) occur where the temperature is below 0°C (-32°F).

EXPANSION AND CONTRACTION

Have you ever found that running hot water over a jar lid made it unscrew easily? This is because things get a little bigger when they get hot – they 'expand'.

Metals expand more than many other materials. It is very important for engineers to remember this when they design bridges. During a hot summer, the metal parts of a bridge expand. To stop it buckling, small gaps are left in the bridge when it is built.

If a metal is cooled it will get smaller, or 'contract'. Telegraph wires are hung loosely so that in winter, when they contract and get tighter, they do not snap.

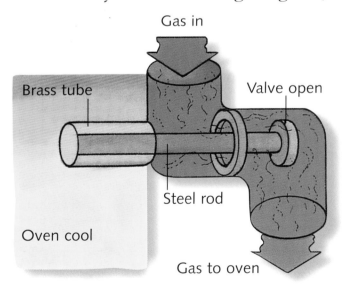

Gas in

Brass tube

Valve open

Steel rod

Oven cool

Gas to oven

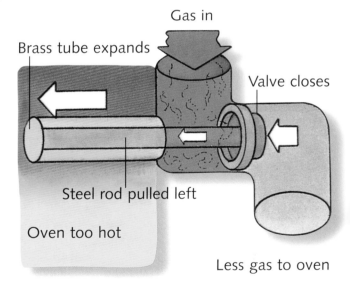

Gas in

Brass tube expands

Valve closes

Steel rod pulled left

Oven too hot

Less gas to oven

Thermostat

Thermostats are used to control the temperature of an appliance, a gas oven, for example. Gas passes through a valve into the oven where it is burned. As the oven gets hot, the brass tube of the thermostat attached to the valve expands.

This pulls the valve in and reduces the flow of gas. When the oven cools down, the brass tube contracts. This causes the valve to open fully again and allows more gas to enter the oven, so it heats up again.

A bridge is built with small gaps between each section so it can expand in hot weather.

INSULATORS AND CONDUCTORS

Heat travels quickly through some substances. These are called 'conductors' and include most metals. Metal feels cold when you touch it because it conducts heat away from your body. Other substances carry heat more slowly and so feel warmer. These are called 'insulators'. Air is a good insulator. Mammals living in cold climates often have thick fur which traps a layer of insulating air around them.

An elephant, however, needs to keep cool. Its big ears provide a large area from which heat can leave its body.

Vacuum flask

A Vacuum flask keeps hot things hot (or cold things cold). The two silvered walls have a vacuum in between them. A vacuum insulates since heat can only travel across it by radiation. The shiny surfaces of the flask absorb little heat, so any heat is reflected backwards and forwards between them. A cork stopper provides insulation at the top of the flask.

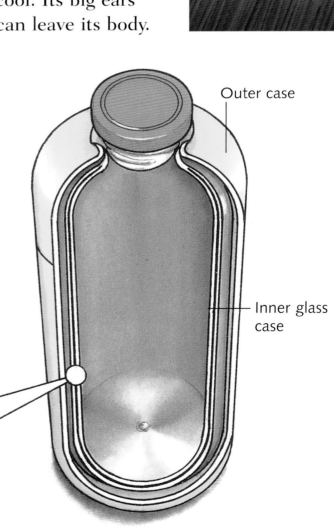

Outer case

Inner glass case

Vacuum

Glass walls

Silvered surfaces

Heat reflected backwards and forwards

People keep warm by wearing clothes that trap pockets of air.

Seals keep warm by having a layer of insulating blubber (fat) and thick fur.

HEAT AND ENERGY IN THE HOME

Energy is used in our homes in many forms – lights and heating, cookers and fridges. Electricity or gas transfers energy to an appliance so that it can do work. Other fuels such as coal and wood are still used in some parts of the world to provide heat and light.

In cold climates, houses use a variety of insulators to cut down on heat transfer to the outside (right). In hot countries, houses have to keep out the Sun's heat. They have thick, solid walls to insulate them and shutters to keep out the sunlight.

Painting buildings white helps to keep out the Sun's heat.

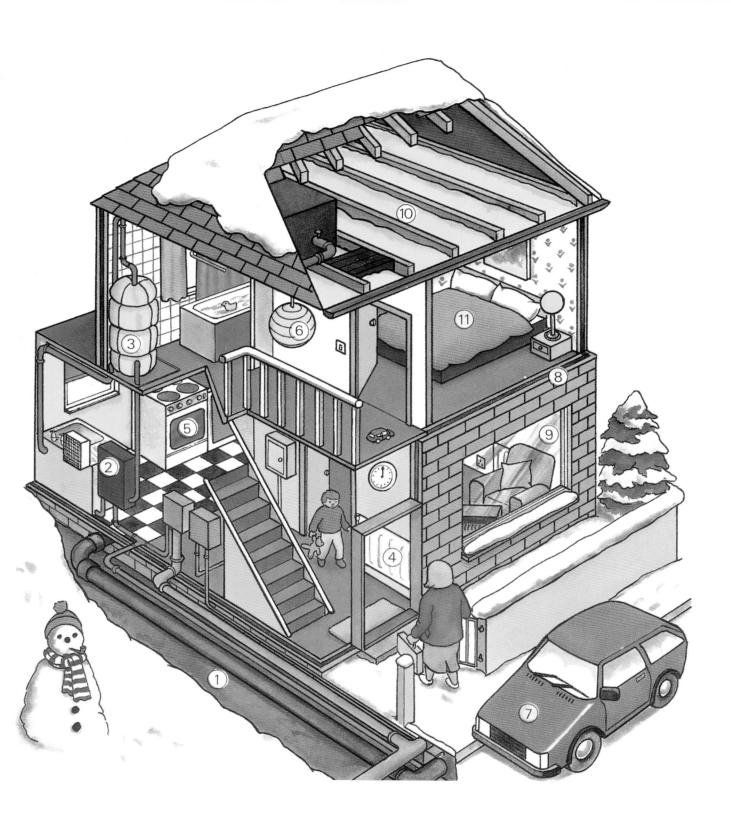

The house is supplied with gas, water and electricity by underground pipes, and sewage is pumped out (1). Some gas is burned with oxygen in a boiler (2) to provide hot water which is stored in an insulated tank (3). Hot water is also used to fill radiators (4). More gas may be burned in a gas oven (5).

Electricity is used to provide light (6). The family car is driven by petrol which burns in its engine (7). Insulating air is trapped between gaps in the wall (8) and between double-glazed windows (9). The loft is lagged for insulation (10) and a duvet (11) provides insulation in bed.

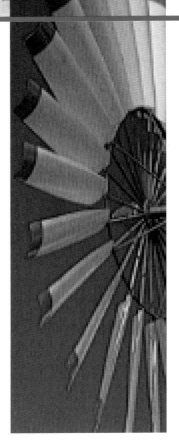

MAKE YOUR OWN WINDMILL

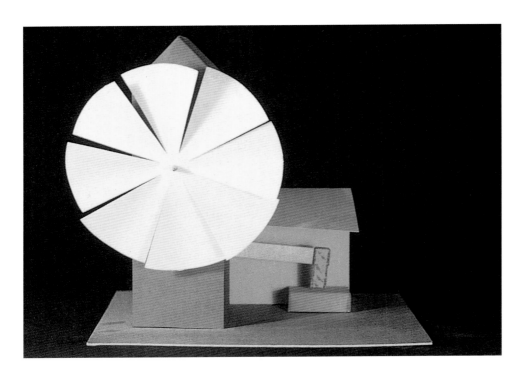

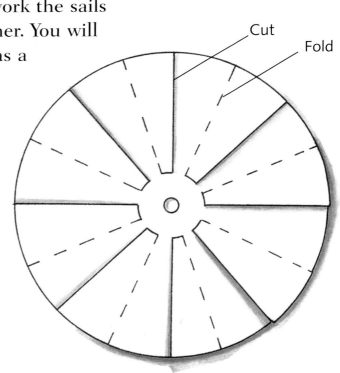

A windmill allows us to use energy from the wind. This one can use movement of air to work the sails and so cause the movement of a hammer. You will need to use a hair dryer or fan heater as a source of 'wind' to drive your windmill.

Cut

Fold

What you need

A clean empty milk or fruit juice carton
Cardboard
Two plastic biro insides
Two thick straws
Scissors

To make the sails, mark out a circle of card as shown. Cut along the solid lines and fold along the dotted ones. The carton will become the windmill's tower. Make a sloping roof from cardboard and paint it if you like.

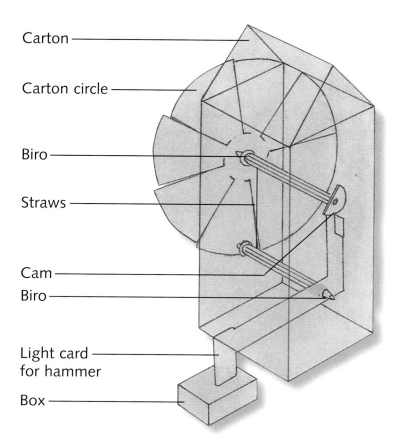

Carton
Carton circle
Biro
Straws
Cam
Biro
Light card
for hammer
Box

Putting it together

Make four holes in the carton and slide the two straws through them as shown. Put a biro through each one. Cut the straw and biro to fit. The sails should be fastened to the upper biro at the front of the tower. Attach a small semi-circle of thick card (the cam) to the other end of this biro. The sails and the cam should turn together.

Now cut a cardboard arm with a hammer-shaped head. About 2 cm from the top, make a cut halfway across the arm. Fold to make a flap which stands up. Attach the arm to the lower biro. When the sails turn, the cam should flick the arm backwards and forwards, moving the hammer up and down onto the box.

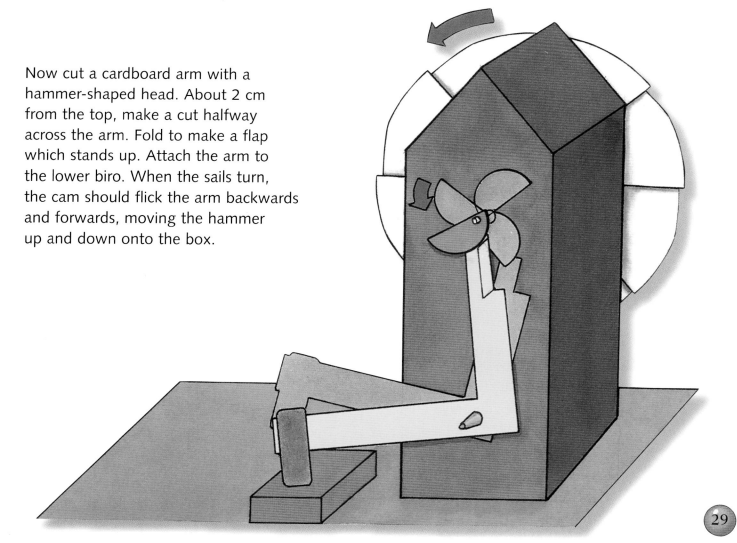

MORE ABOUT HEAT AND ENERGY

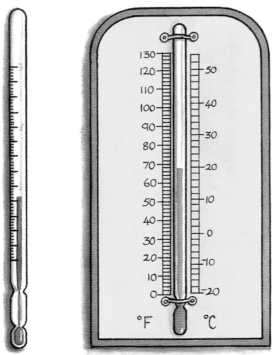

Clinical thermometer

Alcohol thermometer

Alcohol and mercury thermometers

We use many different types of thermometers at home, in hospitals and in laboratories. In colder countries where temperatures are often below 0°C, many outdoor or household thermometers are filled with alcohol. Alcohol has a lower freezing point than water or mercury. A red dye is usually added to the alcohol to make it easier to see.

Digital thermometers are used when high temperatures need to be measured.

Energy and temperature

Imagine holding a red-hot nail by a pair of pliers and dipping it into a bowl of cold water. The temperature of the water would hardly change. However, if a kettle of boiling water is poured into a bowl of cold water, the temperature of the cold water rises. The red-hot nail has a higher temperature than the boiling water but there is more energy in the kettle of boiling water than in the red-hot nail. The amount of energy depends on the temperature and also on how much of the substance there is.

GLOSSARY

Appliance
A piece of equipment which has a particular purpose, for example, a hair dryer.

Cam
A bit of machine. It may change circular movement of one part of a machine into up and down movement of another part.

Carbon dioxide
A gas. A small amount of this is in the air.

Conduction
Conduction is the way in which heat energy travels through a substance.

Contract
When something contracts, it shrinks in size.

Convection
Convection is when heat is moved through a gas or liquid because the heated parts of the gas or liquid move to cooler parts.

Double-glazed
Describes windows made with two panes of glass with a gap between them.

Energy
Something which can do work uses energy.

Expand
When something expands, it swells in size.

Force
A force is something that pushes or pulls on an object.

Heat
A process in which energy is transferred from one place to another.

Insulator
An insulator is a substance that does not conduct heat well. Insulators keep cold things cold and warm things warm. Air is an insulator.

Irrigate
Supply agricultural land with water.

Lagged
Covered in insulating material (that is, material which conducts heat poorly).

Minerals
Chemicals found in the earth. Several, such as magnesium, are necessary for plants to grow properly.

Photosynthesis
A process in which green plants use the energy of sunlight to make sugars from water and carbon dioxide.

Radiation
Radiation is when heat energy is transferred as a ray. Radiation can travel through a vacuum. The Sun travels across space by radiation.

Refined
Separated and purified.

Silt
Mud which has been deposited by water.

Temperature
Temperature is a measure of how or cold something is. The two most common temperature scales are Fahrenheit and Centigrade.

Vacuum
Space in which there is nothing, not even air.

Valve
A device which can control the movement of a gas or a liquid, often through a pipe. It usually only allows movement in one direction.

Vibrates
Moves quickly to and fro.

Work
When a force is exerted on something that moves, we say that work has been done.

INDEX

Photocredits

Abbreviations: l-left, r-right, b-bottom, t-top, c-centre, m-middle

Front cover main, 1, 4tr, 4-5, 6tr, 8tr, 11, 12tr, 18tr, 19tl, 20tr, 22tr, 25t, 26b, 30tr — Digital Stock. front cover mt, 16tr, 19tr, 26tr — Flat Earth. front cover mb, 6b, 13, 17t — Corel. 2-3, 7 — John Deere. 4tl, 6tl, 8tl, 10tl, 12tl, 14tl, 14tr, 16tl, 18tl, 20tl, 22tl, 24tl, 26tl, 28tl, 30, tl, 31t, 32t — Liz Roll/FEMA Photo News. 5tr, 21t, 23 — Photodisc. 9 — Stockbyte. 10tr — Argentinian Embassy, London. 15tr — Johnny R. Wilson/US Navy. 15b — Dan Pavlik/USCG. 19b, 21b, 24tr, 25b — Corbis. 28tr — Peter Fraenkel. 28ml — Cooper-West.